Online Dating For Men: The Basics

CASSIE LEIGH

Copyright © 2014 M.L. Humphrey

All rights reserved.

ISBN: 978-1-950902-50-7

Also published under ISBN 978-1507819272

TITLES BY CASSIE LEIGH

DATING FOR MEN
Online Dating for Men: The Basics
Don't Be a Douchebag
You Have a Date, Don't F It Up
The How to Meet a Woman Collection

DATING FOR WOMEN
Online Dating for Women: The Basics
Online Dating is Hell

DOG-RELATED
Puppy Parenting Basics
Puppy Parenting in an Apartment
Dog Park Basics

COOKING-RELATED
You Can't Eat the Pretty

CONTENTS

Introduction	1
Disclaimer: Target Audience	3
What Is Your Goal?	5
A Moment's Pause: Level Setting	9
Free Or Paid?	11
Privacy	15
Communication Preferences	19
Structured Communication: A Few More Thoughts	23
Level Of Control	25
An Aside: People Lie	31
Specialty Site Or Popular Site?	33
How Many Sites To Start With	37
Just Because She Responds Doesn't Mean She's Interested	39
Another Thought	41
Time to Take A Breather And Summarize	43
Picking A User Name	45
Picking Your Profile Photos	47

Your Profile: What To Say	53
Your Profile: Categorizing Yourself	57
Time To Communicate	63
Who To Contact	65
What If You Don't Get Responses?	67
She Responded: What Now?	69
Red Flags To Watch Out For	77
Checking For Compatibility	73
Communicating Away From The Site	75
Shutting A Match Down	77
When To Meet In Person	79
Choose A Safe First Date	81
Sex	83
When To Have Sex	85
The First Date	87
Conclusion	89

INTRODUCTION

So you've decided to give online dating a try. Maybe a few of your friends found their spouses that way, or you're tired of the bar scene, or you're recently out of a long-term relationship and wouldn't even know where to go to find the bar scene, or maybe you want to tell your mom that you're making some sort of effort to meet someone without actually having to meet them.

Whatever the reason, you want to give this online dating thing a try. And, because we all hate rejection, you'd like to do it the "right way." Well, good on ya. I admire your starry-eyed optimism and resolve.

Unfortunately, you don't even know where to begin. What site should you choose? What should you say in your profile? What pictures should you use?

There are a lot of moving parts to online dating, and hopefully this book will help you with all of those questions and more.

Can you stumble through it alone? Absolutely. You can get started in online dating without spending a dime. Join a free site today and you'll be good to go within the hour.

But if you want to actually find a quality woman, it's probably a good idea to think through a few things first.

I can't promise success—no one can—but I can at least help give you a good solid start.

Online dating requires healthy amounts of persistence, optimism, and luck. But you know the saying, the harder you work, the more luck you'll see.

So let's get started and give you every advantage we can.

DISCLAIMER: TARGET AUDIENCE

Before we go any further, I want to point out that this book is geared towards men. Like it or not, women's and men's online dating experiences are very different and it turns out it's a lot simpler to focus on one group or the other rather than trying to go back and forth.

Also, in this context, we're talking about heterosexual men. I, quite frankly, don't have enough insight into the LGBT experience to do it justice from a dating advice perspective. While some of the chapters will be useful to anyone entering into online dating, I think it may fall apart after that. A man dating a man is not going to have the same issues as a man dating a woman.

(And for all of you that just said or thought something like, "Amen to that," please take a moment to picture me giving you my stare of death before you continue.)

The advice in this book is based on my experience online dating in the United States. If your country has a robust online dating culture, like the U.S., then what I say here may be true for your country as well. But, having tried online dating in a smaller country with a less developed online dating culture, I can say that my experience there was very, very different than my experience in the U.S.

So keep that in mind, too. Don't blindly follow advice if it doesn't work for you.

WHAT IS YOUR GOAL?

The first thing you have to do before anything else is determine why you're doing this. Because your reasons for online dating are going to drive every other choice you make. This is just for you. Tell your friends or mom whatever you want, but be honest with yourself. Because what you want will drive everything from your user name to the site you use to who you choose to communicate with.

Are you looking for lasting love or just trying to find someone to hook up with for a little fun?

If you're just looking for a good time, this whole online dating thing is going to be much, much simpler for you than it is for the person trying to find "the one". Not as easy as it is for a woman looking for sex, obviously, but it's still easier to find someone for a night than to find someone for a lifetime, yes?

If you want sex, you're willing to be open about it, willing to choose sites geared towards that sort of thing, and willing to hustle enough to get to yes, you'll find it.

For a one night stand you basically need someone willing to do what you want to do who doesn't repulse you so much you don't want to do it anymore. For a lifetime love you need someone you're going to like no matter what shit goes down. Lost jobs, cross-country moves, illness, weight gain, depression, aging, dogs, kids, vacations, etc., etc.

Yeah. Pretty easy to see that the standard for one night is a lot less than the standard for a lifetime.

Now, I'm not saying you're going to end up with some hottie. If you want good looks AND sex, well, that's a much harder goal. Especially if you aren't amazingly good-looking yourself. I mean honestly, let's think this one through for a second.

Figure for every ten guys looking to just get some tonight there are two women who want the same thing. That means that each woman gets to choose from at least five possible choices, which means that you have to offer more than those other four guys. Not the time to be shooting for the stars. Let all the other guys aim for that one really hot chick who wants something casual, while you aim a little lower and actually end up with someone tonight.

Just a thought.

Of course, as someone who always advocates at least trying for the best you can get, that's a bit painful to write. You never know when that perfect ten will say yes, so might as well try.

BUT. This is online dating and so many men think that way it can get pretty painful pretty fast. I am by no means a ten, but I get enough of those might as well try messages on some of the sites to almost drive me away from online dating altogether.

So let's do this: Let's say that you will get to "yes" much faster if you're realistic about what you can offer and aim accordingly.

ONLINE DATING FOR MEN: THE BASICS

Enough of that digression. Back to the point.

If you just want sex with someone around your age and willing, it's pretty easy. Be honest about it and find the sites or apps that are known for that sort of thing and then work it until you get a yes. (There's a reason good salesmen usually do well with the ladies.)

If you want lifelong happiness with one special person, it's going to be much more challenging. Not impossible, just challenging.

Online dating is still dating. And a lot of the issues that kept you from finding a partner in the real world are going to keep you from finding someone online, too. But at least with online dating you can see a much larger pool of potential mates and you get to do it at home in your pajamas or when you're standing in the checkout line at the grocery store.

If you're looking for something serious, don't get discouraged. You can find a life partner through online dating. I have multiple friends who are happily married to people they met online.

Just know that finding that special person to spend the rest of your life with will be far more challenging than finding someone to spend a night with.

The men who are most successful at online dating are the ones who are persistent and don't let a few bad dates or non-responses get them down. And who maintain a positive attitude when interacting with potential matches.

Honestly, if you're looking for someone truly amazing and special and you haven't exhausted the friend-of-a-friend referrals and haven't yet approached that cute girl you see every week at rock climbing, I'd suggest doing that first before you wade into online dating. But if you've exhausted all your real world possibilities or like the idea of getting to peruse a woman's info before you take the next step, then online dating it is.

Okay, so back to the main point of the chapter:

Why are you online dating? What do you want?

Sex?

Friendship?

A fuck buddy?

A steady Friday night date that doesn't care who your Saturday night is spent with?

A long-term, but not marriage-minded, committed relationship?

Marriage?

Marriage and babies?

You can find any of the above. You just have to approach it the right way.

Step one is being honest with yourself about what you want. Step two is being honest with others about what you want. (And if you really aren't sure, like a friend of mine wasn't, choose one but be open to women that fall outside of that choice.)

A MOMENT'S PAUSE: LEVEL SETTING

Whether you find someone or not will also depend very much on what you're looking for. If you want a nice, typical, sweet girl of average looks, you can probably find her. If you want an ex-model who's now an astrophysicist, well...that's going to be harder. (Just like in real life.)

Hopefully not impossible. Although, really, how many ex-model astrophysicists are out there?

I feel with men I have to emphasize more this concept of aiming to the right level because with online dating men initiate the majority of the communication. Which means you are the one that drives your online dating experience.

So while you're figuring out what you want out of this, also think about what you can realistically achieve. You will see hot women on these sites. Women that you can message, but who are so clearly wrong for you it's not even funny.

Do you approach them? It's tempting, but I'd argue that you shouldn't waste your time on those kinds of girls.

Let me give you a parallel example.

Most of us are familiar with the concept of applying for college. While it might be great to walk through life saying you went to Harvard, most people don't apply there. Why? Because they take a realistic look at their test scores, GPA, and activities and say, "No way in hell could I get in there. So why waste the time and money to apply?"

Instead they apply to schools that are in range for them whether that's the local junior college, a state school, or some lesser known but highly rated school.

Approach dating the same way. Sure, you can keep going after the Harvards of the dating world and maybe someday you'll get a yes. In the meantime, you're sleeping alone and getting older. And poorer. Because some of those girls might say yes just for the free meal. (Our society fucks up pretty women's heads...and men that want to get into their pants and buy them shit to get there make it worse.)

So focus on what you really want. And if it isn't someone to impress your friends with, aim for something lasting and realistic. Find a woman who is on your level, whatever level that is.

And if you really must go after the Harvards of the world, you better bring something to the table to attract that woman's attention, whether it's looks, money, or an amazing personality. (Or just the ability to not be a completely sex-crazed douchebag.)

Also, if you do go that way, do it with absolute confidence. Do not let her know that you think she's above you. Believe when you approach her that she'd be lucky to be with you. Your confidence may just win her over.

PICKING A SITE OR APP: STEP ONE – FREE OR PAID?

Now that you know what you want from online dating, it's time to pick a site or app.

Ah, choices.

There are so many sites or apps out there and they're changing all the time, so I'm not going to recommend specific ones. I'm just going to give you some general things to think about.

First, you need to decide whether to choose a paid site (like eHarmony or Match) or a free site (like OkCupid or Plenty of Fish).

In my experience, the ones that charge money generally attract more serious users. From what I've seen, the free sites tend to have more men that are less accomplished professionally, less skilled at communicating with a woman, and generally on the younger end of things. Or recently divorced or separated and trying to save money.

Which means that for you, if you're not one of those things, you'll stand out from the crowd. Of course, if you're too much not like that you may raise the question as to whether you're real. I remember seeing a profile on one of those sites for a law firm partner who was incredibly good-looking. I have to admit that, compared to who else was on that site, I wondered if someone hadn't created a fake profile. I passed him by for that reason.

What you need to understand as a man approaching women on one of the free sites is that the signal to noise ratio is insane. Meaning, for every legitimately interesting message a woman receives, she probably receives twenty that make her consider giving this whole dating thing up and just joining a nunnery. It makes your job a lot harder. She will be much more on the defensive on a site like that.

Now, having said that, if you want casual and quick, a free site is probably the way to go. Because a girl looking for casual isn't going to mind a "Hey hawtie, what's up?" message and she'll be on there and off of there so fast that it won't matter what other crap she gets as long as she finds someone to have fun with.

If you're looking for a serious relationship or marriage, then I say spend a little money. The women who are looking for serious are much more likely to be on the paid sites. I had a friend who recently tried online dating for the first time and her choices were eHarmony and Match. She didn't even think about the free sites.

When I've done them—and I have—it's been because I felt like I should be dating, but didn't really want to put any money into the effort so I knew I could slap up a profile and feel like I was making progress without it costing me anything. Not the kind of girl you want to date.

(Having said that, I will say that a friend of mine met her husband on OkCupid. So it can happen.)

In terms of the paid sites, how long should you sign-up for? I say three months.

My male and female friends who were really serious about finding someone (which means working it hard enough to generate multiple dates per week until they found someone) generally managed to do so within ten weeks or so of joining the site.

And, honestly, even if you don't find someone within three months, you'll want to move on to a new site because, even with the bigger sites, the pickings get slim after a while.

However, many of the sites offer ridiculous price discounts if you join for longer. The last site I joined cost $11 a month if you joined for a year or $40 a month if you joined for three months. (They do this because it makes it look like they have more members than they do. It also gives them more matches to send you even if the person they're sending you hasn't been online in six months. Something my friend can attest to after she dated a guy for three months and then went back to the same site for new matches and everyone they sent her had been inactive forever.)

So, free for fun, paid for serious, and if you join a paying site, plan for three months.

PICKING A SITE OR APP: STEP TWO – PRIVACY

Next you need to think about privacy. When you date in the real world, your dating life tends to stay separate from your professional life unless you deliberately let the two mix. Date your co-workers and your personal life becomes everyone's business. Get drunk with your co-workers and hook up with some random person at the bar while they're watching, that gets back to them, too. But spend your weekends at your neighborhood bar with your friends from high school and no one really cares or knows.

Online dating is different. First, some sites make your online dating profile public in order to attract other members. Is that okay for you? Are you comfortable with having your boss, co-workers, or other professional colleagues able to see your profile?

Some of these public sites ask about smoking, drug usage, sexual preference, sexual experience, etc. Would you feel comfortable answering those questions honestly knowing that anyone can see them? (If you don't answer honestly, what's the point? The people you meet on there are not going to be who you want to meet or you're not going to be who they want to meet.)

You still have to think about this with the subscription sites, too. I had a good buddy who was on Match for a long time and they kept suggesting the secretary in our office as a potential match for him. She could see everything he said about himself, which was interesting since he was not-yet divorced when he joined and the fact that he was getting divorced wasn't exactly public knowledge yet.

I once had a match that turned out to be a guy I went to high school with. Another time a site suggested a former co-worker as a potential match.

Are you comfortable having the people in your life see your dating profile? Because if you're going to date online, it will happen.

Think about it now before you have to deal with it in the office on Monday morning or at Thanksgiving with the family.

The other privacy issue you need to consider is what the site reveals about you by the way it's structured.

I don't know of any sites that use your full name, but there are some that show your real first name to other users. (eHarmony, for example.) That's fine for people with names like Jane and Mike, but not so good for people with really unique names.

I have a friend with a unique enough name that you can use her first name and the city she lives in (which most of these sites also show) to find her home address and LinkedIn profile which lists her current employment and the schools she attended.

Maybe you don't think that's an issue. You think, "So what? What if your matches can find you in the real world?" If you like a girl, you're going to tell her those things eventually, right?

Here's the thing. Just like in real life, you will meet some crazy fucking people online dating. (On some days it seems like that's all there is.) Do you really want someone you've never met showing up on your front doorstep because they can't understand why you shut down that match when you two are clearly soul mates?

No? Then think carefully about what you're revealing about yourself and find a site that works within your comfort level.

(By the way, the way to solve this with eHarmony is to know about it when you sign up for your account and provide an initial or nickname when you list your name. As far as I know, once you put in your name it doesn't let you change it, so you have to get this right when you join.)

PICKING A SITE OR APP: STEP THREE – COMMUNICATION PREFERENCES

Okay. So, you're going to pick a site that aligns with your goals and gives you the privacy you need. Next you need to give some thought to how you like to communicate with people.

Some options (like eHarmony) have a structured communication approach. You get to ask three multiple-choice questions, then they answer, then they ask you three multiple-choice questions. Then you get to ask three open-ended questions, then they answer, and ask you three open-ended questions, then ...You get the point.

With those sites, your first few interactions are structured. It's good for men in two ways. First, it's less painful for women to be on those sites because they're not getting bombarded with the whole "hey, hottie" kind of e-mails that some men like to send. (Not you, of course, right?)

Second, it gives you something to say when you reach out to a woman. You don't have to think about something witty to say about her profile, you just choose your three questions and hit send. She's already communicating with you by the time you have to actually form unique sentences, which gives you a little bit of "good karma" with her.

Random aside. They did this study with political signs. They'd go door-to-door and ask if they could put this little sign in the person's window. Most people said yes. It was very small and innocuous. Then they came back a few days later with a gigantic sign to put in the person's yard and asked if that was okay. Most people asked about the gigantic sign first said no. But a decent percentage of the people who had agreed to put the tiny sign in the window said yes, because they'd already agreed to display a sign previously.

Think of these structured communication sites like that. You sent your three questions and she replied. You sent three more, she replied. You sent your must haves/can't stands, she replied. You have three "yes" responses from her before you have to venture out on your own. So even if you screw up that first open communication, she'll still probably respond to you.

The other key thing about structured communication steps is that they're designed to ferret out key differences, so you can weed out bad matches early on.

There are advantages to structured communication. But it can also kill the momentum, destroy any natural chemistry that exists between two people, or mask someone's social ineptitude.

(Also, keep in mind with eHarmony that if you choose to provide your own answer, saying "all of the above" or "A and C" are useless answers, because the person reading your answer can't see what your choices were. And unless they've been doing this a lot, they don't even remember what the choices might have been.)

Back to the disadvantages of the structured approach.

Imagine meeting someone in real life. Instead of getting to just chat with them and let the conversation go where it will, you have to ask and respond to a set of structured questions that don't show your personality and don't let the other person show theirs.

"What are your must haves?"

"Well, I want a man who is kind, funny, and intelligent. What are your must haves?"

"I want a woman who is physically passionate, fit, and kind. What are your can't stands?"

"I don't like men who objectify women."

And so on and so forth.

Yawn.

If you're looking for marriage and babies, maybe the structured approach is better. It lets you address some of those key issues before you get ahead of yourself. If you're looking for tonight's hook-up, it's a definite waste of time and energy.

There are sites that don't put you through that approach, but will still have serious-minded people on them. Your best bet is to ask around.

Do an internet search or two. Not for the sites, most don't tell you enough to make that determination, but for bloggers who review the sites. See what others have to say and decide if that approach will work for you.

STRUCTURED COMMUNICATION: A FEW MORE THOUGHTS

I mentioned above that one of the benefits of structured communication is that it lets you weed out bad matches. Of course, this only works if you actually pay attention to the answers.

Let me give you an example. One of my matches said he doesn't like women who watch TV. I watch a decent amount of it. Says so right there in my profile. He put it on his list of can't stands. I wrote back and pointed out that I watch a lot of it. He kept writing me.

There is no point in using structured communication that's designed to highlight key differences between you and the person you're communicating with unless you actually use it to do so.

On this particular site I tend to eliminate a decent number of matches at the must have/can't stand stage. I don't think I've ever had a man eliminate me at that stage. Not once. Don't do that. Actually read the answers. It isn't about getting through to open communication so you can ask for a date. It's about communicating. Listen to what she says. And don't be afraid to shut it down if it doesn't work.

Also, since we're digressing here. As much as appearance and sex matters to you, do not emphasize it. If a man's ten must-have traits include sexually experienced, sensual, physically demonstrative, and physically fit, I close the match down. Not because I'm anti-sex, but because the man still hasn't grown up enough to realize that there's more to a good relationship than being with a hot woman who wants to have sex with him. And that the time to discuss sex and passion is not when you're communicating online with a complete stranger.

See, men don't go through what women do. So let me try to share with you what it can be like…

From the age of fifteen onward, I had adult men very confidently and openly telling me how sexy I was. Sometimes quite explicitly. Now, when you're fifteen and just got curves, it can be pretty fun to see that men find you attractive. But fast-forward ten years and when that's still all strange men say to you it starts to get old.

That's why women become bitchy in public. Because a lifetime of "I wanta fuck you" gets old. So, let's assume that if you're online dating and the woman hasn't clearly listed religious or moral beliefs about sex, that she's into it.

Yes, I know. There are men who found themselves in sexless relationships that never want to go there again, so *it matters*. I get it. But I'm telling you that your odds of getting to the point with a woman where you have the chance for sex to happen go up if you play it a little cool and focus on other things first.

Just my personal opinion. I'm sure there are women out there who would feel very differently about this. I'm sure there are women out there who live to have strange men tell them how sexy fine they are today.

Do as you will, I'm just warning you why it may backfire on you.

PICKING A SITE OR APP: STEP FOUR – LEVEL OF CONTROL

Okay, you've found a site that aligns with your goals, gives you the privacy you need, and lets you communicate in the way that works best for you.

What next?

Decide whether you want a site that will let you choose your own matches or one that's going to help you find the "right" match for you.

If you're looking for casual, you probably don't care too much about the "right" match. To be physically compatible you probably don't even have to like each other. (And now is not the time to digress into the "be careful who you sleep with because you may end up liking them so much you stay with them even though you hate a lot of things about them" lecture. Although, well, what I just said.)

If you're serious about finding a long-term relationship, it's possible that a site that chooses for you will help you get past certain biases you might have.

You know, like you only go for women who are blonde, between 5'4" and 5'6", and whose names end in –ie.

The benefits of a site that filters matches based upon your personality profile is that theoretically you're only focusing on all those other attributes after they've found you people who are compatible on the emotional/psychological level.

Theoretically.

Now, let's stop and discuss this for a minute.

I've tried a few of these sites and, in my experience, they don't always work as well as you'd like them to. Some, like OkCupid, allow the users to decide whether to use the matching algorithms. They tell each user the percent compatibility between them and their potential match, but you can contact anyone.

In my experience men rarely if ever let a low compatibility score keep them from reaching out to a woman they find attractive. And, since answering the questions that generate the compatibility numbers is optional, most users just skip it, which means that even if it matters to you most women won't have answered enough questions for it to work.

Everyone will be 85% compatible at most because they answered a whole ten questions and only five of those overlap with the ten you bothered to answer.

What could be really helpful in narrowing down possible matches isn't at all. Which is too bad because it's the only site I know of where you can have some pretty freaky preferences and use those matching algos to find other people with the same kinks.

(If you do have some sort of specific preference, then answer the damned questions and pay attention to the answers. And be honest in your answers. I rant about this in *Don't Be A Douchebag*—a book you will hopefully never need to read.)

Some sites, like eHarmony and Chemistry, force you

to complete a questionnaire before you can join and then they use the results to choose matches for you.

What about those sites?

Well, remember that whole discussion about how there are a lot of perfectly decent ordinary folks that do online dating? I think those sites work great for them.

Someone like me? Not so much.

This isn't arrogance talking (although I am arrogant), but I'm just not normal.

I've taken the Myers-Briggs (MBTI) a few times and supposedly my personality type is present in less than 5% of the population. Which, given my experience on those sites, seems pretty accurate. That means that there are a very small number of men that are good fits for me.

If those sites only gave me that handful of matches that were truly compatible, that would be fine. I'd rather have a small number of matches that really work for me than ten a day. Instead, they give me lots of matches that just don't work.

Each time I've taken one of those questionnaires, the site nailed my personality profile and what I'm looking for. I'd read it and think, "Yes, this. This is me and what I want."

And then they'd give me men that didn't meet it.

If you have a unique personality type, expect to have a lot of matches that aren't what you're looking for. And expect that just because the site tells you that someone is compatible with you, that doesn't really mean they are. In my experience, they provide matches when one side or the other will find the match interesting, not when both sides will.

(As an example, if you're a Builder-type on Chemistry, just avoid the Explorer-types. You may find them interesting, but chances are they won't feel the same way...)

What do you do if you are one of those unique personalities? Is it better to avoid the personality matching sites?

Maybe. But, problem is, there aren't going to be more people like you on the other sites. (Unless people with your personality type tend to choose the same kind of parameters so go for the same types of sites in which case just follow your gut about what you like the best.)

At least with the personality matching sites you have a snowball's chance in hell of getting a good match. On the other sites the haystack you're searching through is even bigger and the chance of finding that needle (e.g. match) are really small.

Again, this is assuming what you want is long-term. Short-term, who cares?

Bottom line? Unique personalities need to be prepared to be frustrated by a lack of appealing choices and need to force themselves to stick with it longer than normal folks.

But back to the basic question. Do you choose a site that picks matches for you or choose a site that lets you pick your own matches?

If you choose one of the sites where it's a free-for-all, you are facing more intense competition. Everyone can message that woman that interests you. On the matching sites, the woman "only" gets ten to twenty matches a day, not all of whom will message her. (Although a fairly high percentage do.) On the open sites, she gets as many messages as there are men who saw her profile and liked it that day.

So, more competition.

And, you're much more likely to focus on all the wrong criteria.

Like what? Well, you tell me.

If I gave you a site with a million women on it and told you to enter search criteria so we could narrow it down for you, what would you enter first? If you're a stereotypical guy (and, yes, there are always exceptions you special snowflake you), you'd probably start with: Age. Height. Eye color. Hair color. Body type.

Most men put a premium on physical looks. Nothing wrong with that, but it makes finding what you're looking for that much harder. If you want casual, maybe the best place to start is with someone looking for casual. If you want serious, maybe it's more important that the woman want the same things in life that you do.

Plus, at least three of the items on that list can change. I could go out tomorrow, dye my hair black, get blue contacts, and lose or gain ten pounds in the next month. Far more important to find someone mentally compatible first.

Really, it is.

Even for sex.

Maybe especially for sex.

(I'm not going to elaborate on that one, just think it through. And if you don't get it, well, hm. Maybe you're reading the wrong self-help book...)

On the free sites, there's also such a thing as choice overload.

They've done studies that basically say that having too many choices is worse than having a limited number of choices. If you can only have A, B, or C, you're pretty happy when you get B. If you can have A-Z, then you're comparing B to everything else you could have had and feel less satisfied.

Limited choices help result in long-term relationships. Or making a choice at all.

You don't want to get the "ooh shiny" syndrome and spend months on the site never getting past the first date because there was someone else who looked like maybe they were more interesting and while you were off checking that new girl out you lost the one you'd already found.

If you do go free, do it with focus. Get in, get what you want, and get out.

AN ASIDE: PEOPLE LIE

You have to be careful with online dating because people lie. Many profiles are what you might call aspirational rather than realistic.

If you honestly think that searching for fit women is going to get you size 2 women and nothing else, I'd like to sell you some ocean-front property in Arizona. There might be a few in there. But there'll be a lot of size 10 women who go to the gym five times a week and think that counts. And know that "healthy" probably means slightly overweight. Because who wants to call themselves fat? That's what those other people who weigh fifty pounds more are, not me.

Also be careful of anyone whose age is listed as 29, 39, or 49. They could very well be 30, 40, or 50 and just be lying so they can appear in the lower age bracket searches.

Just like in the real world, people are insecure and most aren't comfortable with who they are. (Don't be one of those people, by the way. Just because others lie doesn't mean you should.)

Always proceed with caution. Even photos can deceive.

PICKING A SITE OR APP: STEP FIVE – SPECIALTY SITE OR POPULAR SITE?

Alright. So, that's the basics.

One, find a site that aligns with your goals.

Two, find one that gives you the privacy you need.

Three, find one that lets you communicate in the way that works best for you.

Four, find one that provides you with the right tools to help find the person you're looking for.

What else?

What about those specialty sites? Should you use them?

Maybe. But remember that the more niche the site, the smaller the population of potential matches. Which is fine if the focus of the site matters to you enough or if that helps you narrow down your choices to a really great population of possibles. But don't assume that it'll work that way.

Let me give you an example.

I recently found an online dating site where you could post about books you liked and find other singles that liked the same books. Perfect for someone like me. I'm a voracious reader and I believe you can tell a helluva lot about someone by what they like to read.

So I checked out the site. There were a ton of men on there who had experienced life-changing transformations after reading *Outliers* by Malcolm Gladwell. Me? I hated that book. I thought the guy covered really interesting topics and then drew poor conclusions based upon unsubstantiated facts. I swore to never read another book by him, which meant I certainly had no interest in dating any man who thought it was the best book he'd ever read.

Interesting site, but obviously not for me. It didn't attract my type of guy. Which is when I realized that, as much as I love to read, most of the men I've really clicked with over the years haven't been big readers. Whatever it is that connects me to the men I like, it's not their ability to discuss the latest bestseller. As a matter of fact, there's no way to kill my mood faster than to have some guy spout off about a book I really liked, because it's rare for me to talk to someone about a book I liked or disliked and have us agree on the details of why we liked or disliked it.

Another example is a site for dog lovers. I love my dog and it would make life so much easier if I could find someone who wanted to hang out at the dog park on weekends or understands why I don't want to leave my dog alone just to go have dinner with a stranger.

But there are different types of dog lovers. I take my pup to the lake to swim and let her roll in the mud. She generally has a handful of leaves tangled in her coat on any given day. Well, a dog-lover site full of men who dressed their Shih-Tzus in pink dresses and went to dog shows wouldn't work for me.

So do your homework before you choose a specialty site. And make sure there are enough choices on there to make it worth your time. If you can, look at some actual profiles before you take the plunge.

I will say that if you're religious-minded, it's probably a very good idea to use one of the sites focused on your religion, because shared religious views help form a stable long-term relationship and most of those sites have enough users to be worthwhile. As a non-religious person, I can say that people like me will usually avoid the religious sites, so you also aren't going to find yourself really liking someone who doesn't share the same fundamental beliefs as you if you stick with one of those sites. (And, trust me, that happens and it hurts.)

PICKING A SITE OR APP: STEP SIX – HOW MANY TO START WITH

I recommend that women just choose one site at first because the level of responses they receive is so overwhelming it just doesn't make sense to try more than one site. For men that's obviously not going to be an issue. (Because, face it, men do 90% of the reaching out on these sites.)

Men can definitely juggle more than one site. BUT. Do not lose your focus. It can be easy to send off a bunch of messages to women and then get some responses and start going back and forth and lose track of when it was you communicated with each woman last.

Me? I shut down a match after a week if I haven't heard from him. I'm not a fan of being Plan B'ed. Either you saw my profile and are interested enough to move towards meeting in person or you're not. And dropping off the face of the Earth for a week tells me you're not.

So join multiple sites if you want, but make sure you don't get in over your head.

JUST BECAUSE SHE RESPONDS DOESN'T MEAN SHE'S INTERESTED

You're not going to like this one…

Ugly truth time. Just because you message a woman and she responds, doesn't mean she's interested in you. Sucks, doesn't it?

Why, you ask, would a woman respond if she's not interested?

A few reasons. Some nice, some not.

She's new to this and feels like she should give every guy a chance.

She's too polite not to respond. It feels rude to ignore you, but she doesn't know how to say that she's not interested so she responds hoping you'll just go away.

She's been told she's too picky, so she's trying really, really hard not to be. Even though you're not her physical type and you said that nasty thing about all women being too emotional (do not say things like that when trying to attract women…) she's going to give it a few messages before she shuts you down.

She likes the attention. She has a profile up to see just how many men message her and gets a thrill from it.

She's on there not to meet someone for real, but to get a free night out. (Those women exist, but don't go into this thinking all women are like that or you will find that your negativity drives off the women who aren't like that.)

It was Tuesday and she responds to all men who message her on Tuesday. (Yeah, that's me being a smartass. Sometimes people just respond for no reason whatsoever.)

The key here is to know that just because you messaged a woman and she responded, that doesn't mean anything. The whole point of this is to take it to the real world, so until you meet in person, you don't have anything real to talk about. (And, even then, you may not because she may just be being polite or really, really trying to be open-minded.)

ANOTHER THOUGHT

I sometimes find it creepy to see that men are checking out my profile. Especially if they do it too often or when I'm online. One of the sites does pop-up boxes in the corner for every guy looking at your profile. I've logged on to respond to messages and had them pile on top of each other in the corner like some sort of zombie attack.

You don't want to be part of that. You especially don't want to be the guy that sees she's online, checks out her photo, and shoots off a message. (Unless this is about sex, in which case it all works differently.)

On the free sites you can get around notifying a woman that you checked out her profile by looking for matches when you're not logged into the site. Do all your match searches anonymously and write down the user names of the women you liked, then log in and message them.

And, unless you're looking for casual, don't message a woman while she's online. You're not the only one doing it and it puts you in a class of guys you don't want to be associated with.

TIME TO TAKE A BREATHER AND SUMMARIZE

There's a lot to consider, but you probably aren't going to go wrong if you stick with the big sites.

Honestly, if it's too much to think about, just try Match your first time out of the gate. It's the all-purpose site with enough members for everyone and a couple of my guy friends have had solid success on there. Not marriage, but long-term dating as well as hook-ups.

If you want casual, I hear Tinder or AdultFriendFinder work well. I would also put OkCupid or Plenty of Fish in that category.

For serious I would say eHarmony and, although I've never used them since I lack strong religious beliefs, Christian Mingle or JDate.

With all sites, here are the key things to keep in mind:

1. Pick a site that aligns with what you want. Free is more likely to be casual, paid is more likely to be serious.

2. Pick a site that meets your privacy needs while realizing that you probably cannot maintain your privacy completely.

3. Only pick a specialty site if you're really, truly passionate about that particular niche and you can see that the type of people on that site are passionate about it in the same way you are.

4. Choose a site that matches how you like to communicate.

5. Choose a site that will give you the right tools to meet someone and, if you have a unique personality type, be prepared for any personality matching algorithms to not be as effective for you as they are for others.

6. Do your homework. Ask friends what worked for them. Find out how a site works before you join it.

7. Remember that people lie and don't assume that they really meet your criteria just because their profile says they do.

That's about it for finding a site. Next, what to do once you find one.

PICKING A USER NAME

Now that you've found a site, you need to think about how you're going to present yourself.

Not every site requires user names, but a lot of them do. And John1972 is going to get a much different response than BBoyBlitz or Lawman.

So, who are you? And how do you want potential matches to see you?

Personally, I think the name with year of birth thing is boring and shows a lack of originality. Honestly, you couldn't think of anything more creative than your name and birth year?

Also, think long and hard before you choose some sort of name like BBoyBlitz. Does that represent who you are right now? Or is that who you were ten years ago? And is the type of woman you're looking for right now the type of woman that will find a guy like that attractive?

Another thing to consider: It's fine to use a name that has some sort of hidden meaning or reference. You know, like WinterIsComing. But if you do that and a woman gets the reference, don't be a schmuck about it and say, "Wow,

I didn't think a woman would get that." Then why did you use it on a dating website?

You are dating. Focus on that fact and choose accordingly. Your user name is one of the many ways you get to market yourself. Use it well.

Another thought. Be careful about using the same user name on your dating profile as you use elsewhere. I had a match at one point who had used the same very unique user name across the Internet. I did a Google search, as you do, and found a number of interesting things he'd said elsewhere that were not at all apparent from his dating profile. Things that made me decide maybe it was time to move on.

Pick a name that you can live with, that showcases your personality, that isn't boring, and that you don't use elsewhere.

Also, stay away from the sexual references unless you're looking for casual or it really does exemplify your personality. ILuvBoobies may make your friends laugh, but will it make the type of woman you're looking for laugh? If no, ditch it. If yes, more power to you.

Always think about your goals in doing this and act accordingly.

Finally, if you are on a website that uses real names, like eHarmony, and you have a unique name then consider listing an initial, nickname, or more common abbreviation of your name that won't be so easy to Google.

PICKING YOUR PROFILE PHOTOS

The next step is to pick your profile photos. This isn't as important for men—you can get away with crappy photos and a woman will still give you a chance—but the better your photos, the better your chances.

Do post a photo. I had a situation the first time I tried online dating where the guy didn't have a photo. I went along with it. I got burned in the end. I will never again communicate with a guy who doesn't have a photo posted.

According to OkCupid, the best photos for guys are ones where they aren't looking at the camera and aren't smiling. And there have been studies that women prefer men who look intense instead of friendly.

However, personally, I like to see a photo of a guy who looks like he'll be nice. So I prefer someone making eye contact with the camera and smiling.

Then again, I wasn't a big fan of *Fifty Shades of Grey* and it seems 90% of women were, so take that how you will.

Whatever you do, I'd avoid professionally-taken photos. You know, the kind with the blue patterned background and soft lighting. Those shots stick out like a sore thumb.

And try to post photos from different times and places. Only posting photos of you in one outfit and five poses makes me wonder what you're hiding. Did you just lose two hundred pounds? Did you used to be a woman? Why do you have no other photos of yourself?

Variety is good.

Now, if you want something more serious and long-term, then you need to think long and hard before posting too many "fun" photos of yourself. If you want a woman to see you as a provider and father of her children, you probably don't want to post a photo of yourself double-fisting shots at a frat party.

And be careful including alcohol in your photos at all. One photo with alcohol is fine. Every photo with alcohol implies that you might have a drinking problem.

You also need to think about the type of person you're trying to attract. If you want someone active and outdoorsy, then post active and outdoorsy photos of yourself. If you want someone who goes to wine tastings and art exhibits, then post photos of yourself in more sophisticated outfits or settings—wearing a suit, for example.

Also be sure the photos you're posting represent who you really are. Don't post that one photo of you doing that one really adventurous thing five years ago if you never actually do adventurous things.

My prime example of this—and maybe it's just because I used to skydive—is the guy who posts a photo of himself walking back from the landing zone after a skydive. He can't post the one of him in the air, because it was a tandem and he was just meat strapped to the front of the guy actually doing the skydive, so he posts the photo from the field. Look, it's pretty cool to have even done a tandem, but if that's all you've ever done, you were a spectator for one day. It's not you. Don't post it to pretend to be cool.

And no matter how good that photo of you with your ex was, don't use it. It's obvious when you're all dressed up and you cut off half of the photo that you must be posting a photo with an ex.

Also be careful of photos of you and one woman. If you decide to use one of those, be very clear in the photo description who that woman is. And then step back and figure out how creepy it is for you to post a photo of yourself with that woman on your dating profile.

(I had a match post about four photos of himself with his sister. It was just odd to me. I didn't write him off because of it, but it did make me pause and was a strike against him. Know you're being judged and plan accordingly.)

The other issue with having other women in your photos is that you might be conveying to your potential matches the type of women you associate with and she may not like it. I know, that's vague. Let me try to clarify.

A friend of mine had an interesting match. But all of the photos in his profile showed women in their 40's who were trying to look like they were still in their 20's. (You know what I'm talking about.) My friend is not that type. She cares about her appearance, but she's not heavy with the makeup or insane with the hair and the last time she wore a short, tight dress that showed everything was...never. So this guy got the axe, because it was clear to my friend that she wasn't going to like his friends at all.

Early on, just present yourself if you can.

I would also avoid group shots. I know, it makes you look social, so there's an argument for including them. But sometimes it comes off looking too party-like, which tips things back into the "just having a good time" category.

Also, the other people in that photo don't necessarily need their photo up on a dating site.

And, if that's all you post, your potential matches may not even know which one is you. If you do post a group shot, DO NOT make it your primary photo. I have a match right now that did that and I've yet to click on his profile to see if I can even figure out which of the five people in the thumbnail photo are him.

You also run the risk that the woman looking at your photo finds one of your friends more attractive. I know that's happened with me a few times. I look at a match's photos and see a photo of him with his buddies and think, "Bummer that guy wasn't my match." Best to avoid that moment.

You want to draw someone in to you. You want them to get your communication, or that e-mail suggesting new matches, see your profile photo, and think, "He's cute..." or "Wow. He's pretty hot..."

You don't want them to be confused or distracted.

Your photos should also be current. Nothing more than a year or two old. I know, I know, you looked so good ten years ago at your best friend's wedding. But they're not going to date the you of ten years ago. They're dating who you are right now, so show them what they're getting.

Nothing worse than showing up for a date and being severely disappointed by what you find because the person lied. (Much better to show up and be pleasantly surprised.)

And, this should go without saying, post photos of yourself, not someone else. (I had a date tell me some woman used photos of her sister. WTF? What is someone hoping to achieve by doing that? You do want to meet this person in real life, right? Well, think that through...)

You should also think about the quality of the photos you post. Personally, I think professionally-taken photos stand out like a sore thumb, but the nicer the photo, the better you look. So think about using a high-resolution camera instead of a crappy phone, avoid harsh lighting, and make sure you're the focus of the photo. (There's another OkCupid blog that discusses this in far more detail.)

Here's what I recommend whether you're looking for casual or serious:

1. Your main photo should be a close-up shot of your face.

2. It should be a smiling photo, making eye contact with the camera, and looking friendly and open to a conversation. OR, if you want to go with OkCupid's advice, it should be a serious photo looking away from the camera. (Show that strong, manly jaw...)

3. You should have more than one photo posted and at least one should be a full body shot. (This isn't as important for men as for women, but let a girl see what she's getting.)

4. Current photos only unless you make it clear that it's an older photo and it's up there to prompt conversation. (Like that trip you took to Tibet ten years ago.)

5. If you're going to break from the above, make sure you're doing something to trigger people's interest so they'll communicate with you.

6. Post photos that will appeal to the type of person you're looking to meet. (And that legitimately reflect your interests. If you want someone outdoorsy, you should probably be outdoorsy, too.)

7. Post quality photos taken under good lighting with a good camera and where you're the focus of attention.

FILLING OUT YOUR PROFILE: PART ONE – WHAT TO SAY

Alright, so you have a site and photos. Now it's time to say something about yourself.

Let's eliminate the easy one first. If you want something casual, then you don't need to say much. Hell, you're a guy, you're going to be the one reaching out to the women, you may not need to say anything at all. Just have a good photo and pick the right kind of girl.

(What is the right kind of girl? Lots of selfies, fish lips, boob shots, group photos with lots of alcohol and large groups of partiers, and says she likes to have fun.)

For those who want something serious, it's a little trickier.

DO NOT make any statements about women as a group.

Let me give you an example. eHarmony now has this thing where they ask you questions and then they tell your match how many you agreed or disagreed on. One of those questions is, "Do you think women are too emotional?" It doesn't say some women, it implies all women. And there are men, looking to date women, that answer this question, "Yes."

Think about that for a second. You don't know me. You want to date me. And you've just told me that you think all women are too emotional. My reaction? You can kiss my ass. Next.

And, yes, ironically, that may be the reaction of a woman who is too emotional. But, as you should know, insulting women as a whole is generally not the most successful dating strategy.

Be careful in whatever you say or whatever you answer that you aren't giving women a reason to move on to the next guy. Because there is a next guy.

Harsh truth of online dating: Women get approached multiple times per day. Men have to do most of the approaching. For men, it's a bit like preparing for a job interview. Put your best foot forward.

(And this may change as you get older. My grandma says competition for the remaining single, breathing men when you're over sixty is something fierce. Women swarm these guys when they show up at her widower's group. But unless you're already there, you have to make the good impression for now.)

So no negativity towards women, okay?

Include things that will spark conversation. And try to be unique about it. Saying you watch football each Sunday, while true, isn't going to make you stand out from the crowd. Saying you play jai alai on the weekends will.

Try to mention whatever you like that isn't what everyone else and their mother likes.

And I think demonstrating a sense of humor is always a good thing. Women love men who can make them laugh.

I've seen some people advise that you don't put too much text, but I say be yourself. If you like to put a lot of text in your profile, put a lot of text. But don't feel like you have to. Short and sweet will work, too.

(Oh, and spell check and grammar check while you're at it, please.)

And, remember, privacy. Don't put things in your profile that will let someone track you down in real life. Be generic rather than specific. I wouldn't post a photo of your home or talk about where you like to go hiking. Protect yourself for now. This is more of an issue for women, I think, but men can be stalked too.

Also, watch the bragging. With the photos and with the text. That may work for a certain type of girl, but it can come off as desperately insecure to others. If you're entire profile is "I make money, see? Here's my boat and my house and my fancy car and my..." you're either shallow and have nothing else to offer or you don't realize that women want more than that.

Quiet confidence is good. Desperate showmanship, bad.

FILLING OUT YOUR PROFILE:
PART TWO – CATEGORIZING YOURSELF

All sites want to categorize their users. Some of those choices make a lot of sense. Are you male or female? Are you looking for someone who is male or female? Those types of questions are necessary and easy to answer for 99% of the population.

But most sites go past that. What is your religion? What is your ethnicity? What is your income? What is your education? What is your star sign?

Not only that, but how do you want your potential mate to answer those questions? And how important is it that they answer that way?

Not so easy anymore is it?

Well, let's talk about a few of those.

RELIGION

This is a very easy question to answer if you have a clear-cut religious belief. One of my very good friends is Jewish and there was no doubt in her mind when she went looking for a husband that he needed to be Jewish as well. A good friend of my brother's is also Jewish. He ended up marrying a non-religious woman from Taiwan who converted to Judaism to please the parents. I recently went on a date with a guy who listed himself as spiritual but not religious even though he grew up Jewish.

For someone like my friend, filling out those questions is easy. You say you're Jewish and that you want someone who is also Jewish. (Or, better yet, if you're like my friend, put all of your mother's and grandmother's friends to work rooting out every single Jewish woman they know and skip online dating altogether.)

For someone like my brother's friend or the guy I dated, it's more complicated. If you're religious but not strongly enough to care whether your partner is, or strongly enough for it to impact your lives together, do you list it? It matters to some, it doesn't matter to others. If you list yourself as a certain religion and then end up with matches who were looking for that religion, are they going to be disappointed by your level of observance?

I was raised Christian, but only go to church for weddings and funerals (and try to avoid both as much as possible), but I'm also not a fan of people who are openly atheist because I think it's a bit arrogant to assume that you can firmly conclude that there isn't a higher power. But I'm also not spiritual in the sense that I feel there's some spiritual energy connecting all of us. So for me, there's never a good category to choose.

What am I? Other? Not religious? Spiritual? What I end up picking depends on my mood at the time.

And I keep that in mind when I'm setting parameters for what type of mate I'd be willing to accept. There might be a not-very-Christian man who chooses Christian who could be my perfect match. Or maybe it's the spiritual but not religious guy. The wider the net you cast, the more choices you get. But the more mismatches as well.

If you do choose certain religions as acceptable and you aren't that religious, be alert to signs that the other person is very much a believer in the religion they've listed and be clear as soon as possible that you are not.

ETHNICITY

This is another fun one. I tend to approach this one from the "what do people see" perspective. Look at my photo and you see a white woman. You don't think mixed or multi-ethnic, you just think white. Truth of the matter is I have all sorts of different ethnic groups flowing through my veins. But I don't think that's what potential mates care about. I think they care about the woman they'll be seeing every day and introducing to their friends and family.

I also think they care about background and cultural traditions. My upbringing was also very white. Sure, we had more Christmas dinners that were Mexican food instead of ham or whatever it is normal white people have for Christmas, but all in all my upbringing was standard white-person upbringing.

So that's what I choose. And then I keep an eye out for someone who really, really wanted someone white. In the areas where I've lived, that's never been an actual issue, but it could be, so be aware of what the person you're with says.

In terms of who you want as a match, well, that's up to you. I had a friend who threw the net very wide and was open to any ethnicity. She really hit it off with a guy who was from a very different ethnic background than her. Seemed to work. Except when she thought long-term. Then she wondered what would happen when they had kids because they wouldn't look like her.

Gut check moment. I'm sure one or two people reading that just flinched. But it's a valid issue for some people and you need to know if it's one for you.

Now, maybe my friend would've grown past that little moment of whatever you want to call it. But I think it's better to think these things through before someone's heart is on the line.

Ask yourself: Would I be comfortable being seen in public as part of a couple with someone of this ethnicity? Would I be comfortable introducing someone of this ethnicity to my family? To my friends? Would I be comfortable having a child that was half this ethnicity? How would my family react to my dating someone of this ethnicity?

Ugly questions to ask yourself in this PC world of ours, but valid ones. Many people are fine being friends with members of different ethnic groups. But marrying someone of a different ethnicity? Well, not everyone is there yet. If you're not, don't waste your time or the other person's by pretending that you are.

And if you're part of an ethnic group, ask yourself if you want to run into that shit. Sure, you may be open to dating anyone, but do you really want to help that person work through all the hidden landmines they don't even know exist in their world until they start dating you?

AGE RANGE

Men are the funniest on this one. I've seen multiple men that list the age range they're looking for as anywhere from two years younger to twenty years younger than them. Haha. You wish. I mean, sure, some men can pull this off. But are you really, truly saying that you can't stand the thought of dating a woman your own age?

I'll tell you, even when I'm in the acceptable age range for a guy like that, I tend to blow him off. Do as you will. If it's that important to you that you date younger, then do so, but I would encourage you to take any age range you think is acceptable and expand it just a bit.

Personally, I'm far more accomplished than most men my age, so I find it difficult to view younger men as equals that I would want to date. But I have to leave room for the possibility that there will be that exception to the rule, so I allow matches as much as eight years younger.

And be honest about your own age. Please. And, no, explaining that you lied about it in the profile is not being honest about it. I know, it's tough, but it is what it is and you don't want to start a relationship off with lies. At a bar you can just not answer the question. Online it's mandatory and one of the first facts that the sites provide about you.

Another thing to consider is that your age is about more than your appearance. It's about your cultural references—I grew up on G.I. Joe and Strawberry Shortcake. A girl five to ten years younger than me probably didn't. And it's about where you are in life. If you're forty-five, that is a different place than thirty-five. It's not quite the cliff it is for women, but there are some major mental adjustments men go through when they hit that big 4-0.

Just be honest about it. Seriously.

INCOME

I don't know why any site asks this question. I find it offensive. And one I just joined doesn't even let you refuse to answer.

I expect the temptation is quite high for men to lie

about this. In our society your value and worth as a man is often tied to your ability to earn money, so who wants to choose the low range, right?

But be honest about it. You think a woman won't be able to tell if you lied, but I can tell when I'm out with a guy who doesn't make as much as me. So can my friends. I had a friend recently date a guy for a few months and she knew she probably earned twice what he did even though they never told each other what they made. It was obvious from where he lived, what he drove, how he talked about money, what he wore, etc., etc.

What to list? For most people, this will be easy. You have a salary and maybe a bonus and they come out to around $X every year. For someone who is self-employed like myself, it's a helluva lot harder. The income I earned this year is five times the income I earned last year and half the income I earned five years ago. And next year, unless I change something in my current plan, I may earn next to nothing.

What number should someone like me choose? I went with the number most representative of my professional experience and place in life. A number that I have earned and that is comparable to what I would earn if I accepted a salaried position tomorrow.

I could've gone higher, but it would've been a stretch to do so. I would encourage you to choose an honest number that is in line with what you have earned and may earn again and to tip towards a higher number if you're right on the edge of a range.

EDUCATION

This one's very straight-forward in terms of what you list. Either you have a degree or you don't. (And three credits shy of a degree is not having a degree. Honestly, if I were looking for a match I'd be far more judgmental of the person who stopped three credits shy of graduating but put down that they had a degree than I would be of the person who never went.)

If you're tempted to weigh this one heavily in terms of finding matches, ask yourself, why does her education matter to you? Do you see it as a proxy for achievement, because it's not.

I say ignore education. Unless, of course, you come from one of those families or social groups where people have to have certain credentials in order to be accepted. If that's the case, I think you should skip online dating and use friends-of-friends or a matchmaker to meet someone because those groups look for far more than just the degree.

STAR SIGN

Should you use bizarre criteria to look for a mate? You know, like star sign?

I'm a rational, practical person and that side of my personality says, "Hell, no." But I have this great book that tells you how compatible you are with someone based upon the week of your birth and the week of their birth, and it has yet to be wrong.

So, do as you will, but if some girl comes along and you feel "it" don't pass her by just because she's a Gemini.

TIME TO COMMUNICATE

You're ready to go. You've posted the photos and completed your profile. Time to let 'er rip.

This is when being a guy sucks. Because chances are, unless you are really, really lucky or really, really amazingly attractive, you're going to have to do all the heavy lifting. You'll have to look at profiles for potential matches and reach out to them.

Which leads men to do a few stupid things. (Do not do them.)

Like the one-liner. The "Hey, what's up?" or "How you doin'?" Now, this could work if all you want is a casual hook-up. Message enough of the right kind of girl and you'll get a response. But if you want serious? (And by serious I mean more than one date...) Skip the one-liner. Especially on the free sites. It happens to women so often it doesn't matter how amazing you are, she will blow right past that message and move on.

Another stupid one is the copy and paste. This one takes a little more effort, but is still a no go. You think to yourself, "I don't want to have to write a new message for every single woman. It's all the same crap anyway. I'll just write one message and send it to every girl." And you do. "Hi, I'm John. I'm 35 and looking for a woman who likes long walks and romantic dinners. Is that you?"

I've seen copy and paste messages that were three or four paragraphs long. Don't do this. If you must use one, at least personalize it. But the fact of the matter is that almost every single copy and paste message comes off as stilted. Because it isn't part of a dialogue. You didn't read her profile, react to it, and respond. She said something, you ignored it, and you said something else that you could've said to any of twenty people.

It doesn't work well. It also doesn't work because if she does respond to that first message, chances are your follow-up response will be so out of synch with the first message that it'll be completely obvious at that point that you were just shooting off as many first messages as you could.

Again, I think the job application analogy works here. This is you sending in your résumé. You are better off applying for a smaller number of jobs (contacting fewer women), but tailoring your résumé to each of them (sending personal messages) than you are mass-mailing one standard cover letter and résumé (the copy and paste message to every woman who looks even close to interesting.)

Focus your efforts.

So if you do skip the one-liner and the copy and paste, what should you say?

It doesn't have to be much. Pick something in her pictures or her profile that interests you and comment on it. And then ask a question. "I see you like to watch *Peaky Blinders*. That is so cool. I didn't know anyone else out there watched that show, too. Who's your favorite character?"

Done.

You've told her you saw her profile, that you read it, that she in particular interested you, and you've given her something to respond to.

Keep asking questions with every response you send her. Always give her something she needs to respond to. It's playing on her sense of politeness. You can blow off a message where someone says, "Nice picture." It's much harder to do when they say, "Nice picture. Where was that taken?"

Always ask a question. Always make it personal.

WHO TO CONTACT

Ah, the million-dollar question. I wish I could keep men from looking at profile pictures before they decide who to contact.

Why? Because men are blinded by beauty. Maybe not all men, but a very high number. And I have seen my guys friends put themselves through more torture and suffering because of this...

But you're going to look, aren't you? Fine. Try to be a little open to women who don't fit your ideal. Hair color? Can change. Eye color? Can change. (Not as often, but it can.) Weight? Will change unless this is just a short-term thing. Especially if you go the marriage and babies route.

So look past the picture. And please read the profile. I know, that's a lot of time and effort to put in if the woman has a lot of text in her profile. But it's worth it. Because if you smoke and she says, "No smokers," you're better off moving on now. Or no drugs. Or no cats. Please. Some things really are not negotiable.

Whatever she listed in her profile was important enough for her to risk receiving fewer matches because it matters to her. So respect that and move on if you aren't what she's looking for.

Otherwise, look for women who are interesting to you. And keep in mind that if there's a huge disconnect between who you are and who she is, that's probably not going to work. I like to hike and get outside, but I'm not Miss Fitness. And yet I get messages from marathoners who like to ski and go to the gym six days a week and want a fit woman. I list my hobbies as watching TV, why are these guys messaging me?

It all comes back to the photo. Don't do that to yourself or her, okay? You'll find someone you really want to be with a helluva lot sooner if you focus on what she's saying and put less weight on what she looks like.

One more thought. Try not to judge a woman for her photos. I saw some article recently where a guy made a nasty comment about women who post a photo they took of themselves in the bathroom mirror. You know, along the lines of, "Don't you have any friends?" Think about it this way: That woman isn't polished at doing this. She's new to online dating and won't be as jaded as some other women.

As a matter of fact, she may be your best possible match right now. Think about it…

WHAT IF YOU DON'T GET RESPONSES

First, did you listen to me about avoiding the one-liners, copy and paste messages, and personalizing what you say? Did you also listen about not focusing on the photo? If every woman you message is a '10+', you have a lot of competition and she may not have the time to respond to you because you just can't compete with the other guys she's hearing from.

When I join a new site, I get around twenty messages in that first day. I've heard of women getting up to sixty. If you are going after a woman every man is going to want you better have great photos and an amazing first message to stand out from the crowd. (Let's think the job application analogy again. What do you bring to the table that makes you worth the interview?)

Have a trusted female friend look at your photos. I had one guy who messaged me and his photos were horrible. He looked pissed off and angry in each one. And I think they were all selfies, too. My brother is one of those guys who never smiles in a photo, so I get it. You don't have to smile, just don't look like a death row inmate.

In fact, you may need to take pictures just for your dating profile. If so, do it. Grab a beer, a good camera, a few changes of clothes, and have a good friend snap some realistic photos of you relaxed and enjoying yourself. Go for a hike if you need outdoorsy photos. Whatever it takes.

I'm convinced that pretty much anyone can take a flattering photo. It's just a question of how many bad photos you have to take before you get a good one. When I was eighteen, I swear nine out of ten photos I took looked great. (Especially since that was in the film camera days and you only had so many chances to take a photo.) Now? Maybe one in forty looks good (thank God for digital cameras), but I can still get a good photo if I take enough of them. You can, too.

If you don't have any good photos and don't want to ask a friend, sit down with a remote control and a video camera that lets you take photos and shoot a couple hundred of them. (That's how I got my blog photo.)

Seriously. Do it. Women are more forgiving about looks than men, but they'll still respond better to an attractive man than an unattractive one.

If you're not getting responses also make sure that your profile, user name, and photos are in synch. I had a guy message me with a user name about rapping, photos of him hangin' in the club, and a profile that talked about how he was a real estate developer. It didn't fit. It didn't make sense. The profile interested me, but the photo and user name turned me away.

Here's the thing: Women generally have enough choices that they can be picky. They're looking for reasons to say no, not yes, to get things down to a manageable level. Remove reasons for them to walk away.

If that doesn't fix it, then it's time to think outside the box.

Be quirky. Be unique. Be bold. Be memorable. Stand out from the crowd.

Everyone on these sites is trying to present themselves in the most flattering light, so what can you say that's real and genuine and will make a woman stop and give you a shot?

If you're not getting responses, what do you have to lose? Try it. If nothing else, you'll show confidence and that's a very attractive quality to most women.

(Note: I did not say arrogance, I said confidence.)

SHE RESPONDED: WHAT NOW?

Well, time to write back.

We talked about this a bit above, but we'll go over it again.

What should you think about when you respond?

First, be yourself. I know the world of online dating is full of people who aren't being themselves, but if you want something real out of this, you need to be who you are from the start. Do you really want to fake who you are for the rest of your life? No. So don't do it now.

Be who you are. If a weird *Supernatural* reference pops into your head, include it. If you want to quote the latest Pitbull song, do so. Want to reference Debussy? Do it.

Second, remember that you're courting someone. I know, old-fashioned term, but good concept. You want to impress her enough that she's willing to meet you in real life. Don't insult her (unless you can do so in a flirting way). Don't argue with her. Don't correct her.

Keep your messages focused on getting to know her and letting her get to know you.

Don't complain to her about your life. Be positive.

Think back to your best dates or most memorable conversations. What were those like? Fun, interesting, engaging? Do that.

Next thing you need to understand is that you probably aren't going to have a 100% success rate. One reply does not equal a date. It equals a "didn't yet find a reason to say no." So keep that in mind. Until you get to the second date, you're still in that "looking for a reason to say no" category.

If a woman doesn't reply to your next message, that's okay. Just move on. Don't take it personal. She could've found someone else. She could've reacted to something you said that has everything to do with her and nothing to do with you.

It doesn't matter. She wasn't the one. Next.

What else should you do? As I said above, give her a reason to write back. Ask questions.

Be complimentary (but not overly complimentary). Try to focus your positive comments on what she's done or who she is, not what she looks like.

Share similar experiences if you have them.

Find common interests.

Now is not the time to figure out if she'd be willing to stay home and raise your babies. Make sure you like her first. And that she likes you.

And remember that you're still strangers to each other. Don't get too comfy. Don't start acting like you've been together for months.

What does that mean? Don't talk to her about cuddling on the couch together. Or about how you had to soak in the tub for an hour because you hurt your shoulder over the weekend.

Keep it appealing and remember that you're still getting to know each other.

Also, still protect your privacy. Don't tell her that you work at the Merrill Lynch office on H Street. Tell her you work downtown and are in financial services. You don't need her being able to find you in the real world.

Now, while you're communicating, you also need to be assessing this girl for more than just "are we compatible." You need to be looking for red flags that she is someone you need to avoid. Like what? Well...

RED FLAGS TO WATCH OUT FOR

What do I mean by red flags that a girl is someone to avoid? I'm sure you'll come up with a few that I can't because I haven't been there myself, but let's see...

1. DRAMA

You've only exchanged three messages and she's already had a mini-meltdown on you about something minor. Or she told you about this one time when she was at the store and someone wouldn't serve her and she threw a drink in their face. Or...

You know this girl. We all know this girl. She's not worth it. You might like the ups and downs, but really, best avoided. Casual or otherwise. You can do better.

2. SHE HAS ADDICTION OR DEPRESSION ISSUES

This one's trickier. I, personally, try to avoid dates who have or have had addiction or depression issues. I don't think it's something you get over. I think it's something you manage to handle, but that means that you are never truly free of it.

Now, there are many wonderful people in this world who have overcome addictions or depression and are living perfectly happy, healthy lives. (My father was one.) There are also many people who have relapsed.

I want someone who can hold it together when the shit goes down—when we both lose our jobs and they're going to foreclose on the house and his mother is in the hospital and my brother is in a car accident. When that happens I want a guy who can keep it together and get through it, not someone who is quite likely to be facing the temptation to drink again or who spirals into a deep depression so I have to deal with him as well as everything else that's going wrong.

The hardest ones to spot are the ones that have a problem, but don't yet realize it. Where do you draw the line between someone who likes to go out and have fun and someone who has a drinking problem? Hard to tell sometimes. But if your gut tells you there's something wrong, trust it and move on.

3. SHE'S NOT WHAT SHE SEEMS.

Beware the woman who seems too good to be true. If you're asking yourself, "how could I possibly be lucky enough to have attracted this woman?" proceed with extreme caution and make sure to meet her in person as soon as you possibly can. She may very well be a guy named Boris who lives in the Ukraine and wants to borrow some money from you.

Keep an eye out and don't trust everything anyone tells you until you've seen it for yourself.

You aren't dating your cousin's best friend here. You're meeting someone with no connection to you or your family or friends. They could be anyone. So just play it a little cool.

And don't agree to reship an unopened package for them or to loan them money.

CHECKING FOR COMPATIBILITY

I covered it a bit above and I'll cover it again even though you may still not listen to me.

It isn't all about the picture. Just because she's attractive doesn't mean she's a good fit for you.

Look past the pretty pictures and ask yourself if this woman is someone you could spend a significant amount of time with. I had a buddy meet some woman online dating who he absolutely detested. They dated for six months. Why? Because she slept with him and it was pretty good and he liked having sex.

I think most men have done that at one point in their lives. It happens, but really, don't go there.

Why? Because while he was in that six-month relationship it's possible that a great woman who would've also slept with him came and went and he missed her. Fast-forward ten years and he's still single and looking and those six months aren't exactly a fond memory.

Ask yourself: Will this woman make my life better? Will I be happier if I'm with her?

If the answer is no, then move on to the next woman. It is possible to find someone who is both attractive and likeable.

And if all you care about is that a woman is good-looking and you don't want anything deeper or more meaningful, fine. That can work. There are women out there that want something as limited in their relationship. (Usually the arrangement is money for looks.) Those women are out there and it can make a great long-term partnership if you both want the same thing.

But if you find a woman who wants a man who's compatible on all levels and will accept and love her no matter what happens in the future and you know you'd dump her if she gains twenty pounds, you'll eventually destroy her and that's just not a nice thing to do to someone else. Move on.

Remember, even though this is online, you're still dealing with a human being on the other end of that computer.

Back to the point: Look past the photos and figure out if there's any real compatibility there or not.

COMMUNICATING AWAY FROM THE SITE

Messaging back and forth on the various sites is pretty easy. It's like any conversation, except via website.

But I know some men like to communicate via e-mail or want to talk on the phone—especially on the paid sites. That can be tricky. You're asking someone to let you into their life. Do it too soon and they're liable to blow you off.

Spend too much time e-mailing and texting and talking on the phone before meeting in person and they're likely to lose interest.

The nice thing about using an online dating site is that you can message with someone, decide you're not interested, and just end the conversation without having to deal with any sort of awkward follow-up e-mails, phone calls, or texts.

If you take things to your personal e-mail account or give out your phone number, you may have to deal with that fallout. Do you want some chick texting you five times a day because you blew her off?

If you are going to give out an e-mail address, think about setting up a new one just for dating. A friend of mine gave her e-mail to some guy and he friended her on Facebook before they'd ever even gone on a date because he used her e-mail to find her account.

So not cool.

Don't do that.

As with all of this, find where you're comfortable. Just remember that these sites are set up, in part, to provide you with a safe environment to meet someone. If you step outside of that environment, you are taking on additional risk. You have to if you really want to meet someone, just be smart about it.

SHUTTING A MATCH DOWN

Sometimes you'll communicate with a girl who seems promising, but it never seems to come together. She may be your most attractive match or your most interesting one or the only one of the bunch that likes karaoke. Whatever it is, you really like her.

But when you try to suggest getting together, she blows you off. Some of this may just be your level of comfort versus hers. But if it keeps happening, you have to question whether it's worth your time to keep going.

Me? I hate talking on the phone or texting and usually use Skype with the camera turned off, so some guy who suggested that would probably be ignored. Or I'd come back with the suggestion to just get together.

So, before you give up, try suggesting something different. If you suggested getting together and she wasn't keen, see if you guys can chat on the phone. If you suggested the phone and she didn't want to, just ask to get together.

Try to move it forward. If you can't, move on.

What if she's one of those that disappears for days at a time? You message back and forth for a few days and then you don't hear from her for a week. Or two. What then?

In this connected world, it's really not true that someone who wants to reach you can't do so in the space of two weeks. If that happens, it's a choice she's making. Other things in her life are more interesting or more important than reaching out to you.

Cut her loose and move on.

I know, she seems great. But chances are the girl has Plan B'ed you or just isn't that interested and doesn't know how to tell you.

What do I mean by Plan B'ed you? That's when a girl thinks you're somewhat interesting, but not as interesting as this other guy she's talking to. So she tries to string you along while she decides whether things with the other guy are going to work out. If they do, she disappears and you're left wondering what happened. If they don't, she turns her attention back to you until someone else new and shiny distracts her again.

You don't want to be with a girl who sees you as her second choice or her fallback plan. Move on and find a girl who thinks you're absolutely amazing.

And don't do this to women. If you're not that interested, cut her loose.

WHEN TO MEET IN PERSON

So, when should you go on a date with a girl you've met online?

Sooner is probably better than later.

I tend to drag things out a bit because I don't want to meet up with a guy who turns out to be a psycho. Another friend of mine was out on first dates within a few days of joining a site.

If you communicate for too long without meeting up in person, the conversation tends to die off after a while. She has other options and you do, too, so if you aren't immediately interested she'll look elsewhere.

I also had at least one situation where the guy got a little too cozy about our e-mails and was suggesting a first date curled up on the couch in his basement watching movies. And another where he started telling me about his back aches and pain medicines. You don't want to go there, so meet up with her before you get too comfy, cozy.

Also, if you let the messaging back and forth go on for too long you may get so tied up with what you think this girl is that you fail to see who she really is. You have this beautiful picture in front of you and you imagine all sort of things that just aren't true. Only way to pop that bubble is to confront it with reality, which is best done sooner rather than later.

Remember, people do lie. For all you know, everything you see in that profile is bullshit. And even if it isn't, there's this thing called in-person chemistry that matters more than most of us are willing to admit. A girl can seem great online and then you meet her in real life and it falls flat.

So exchange a few messages to make sure she's not insane and then agree to meet up.

It's okay. That's the point, right?

CHOOSE A SAFE FIRST DATE

I advise women to be careful on their first date. You're a stranger to her and, unfortunate as this may be, women are more likely to be the victims of violence from a situation like this than men. So your role is to make her feel safe by suggesting a first date that doesn't come off as creepy. Like what?

1. MEET SOMEWHERE PUBLIC

Don't have her come to your house. Don't go to hers. Don't suggest meeting at the end of some remote trailhead for a hike.

2. CHOOSE A DATE THAT ALLOWS EITHER ONE OF YOU TO LEAVE WITH EASE

Don't go on a boat cruise. Don't fly her to another city in your private jet. (Haha.)

3. WATCH YOUR ALCOHOL OR DRUG USE

We each have our personal limits on this, but this is a stranger, and it might behoove you to stay aware of your surroundings and what's happening.

* * *

Those are the biggies. Basically, don't come off creepy and don't suggest something that isolates or threatens her. And don't make a concerted effort to dull her senses. If she wants to drink, fine, but don't be the guy pushing drinks on her or refilling her glass.

If you make it through three hours and it's going well, then let the date go where it may. But start off in a safe space and let her be the one to suggest taking it somewhere more private.

SEX

You met someone online, you've hit it off, and now...You want to have sex.

First, think about your sexual safety. I'm not your mom, but I'm going to act like it for a minute. If you're going into online dating and you don't have strong moral or religious reasons for waiting to have sex, chances are that will be on the table at some point.

Do you have condoms? If not, buy a pack. You don't have to carry them with you for use on a moment's notice, but know that you have them and know where they are and if things are headed in that direction, steer the activity to where you can get them.

Now, maybe you don't like condoms. (Shock.)

If you're not using condoms, how are you protecting yourself from sexually-transmitted diseases? (Or is it sexually-transmitted infections these days? I'm showing my age, aren't I?)

Whatever you call them, STDs or STIs, how are you ensuring that you don't walk away from this experience with herpes or crabs or syphilis or whatever else is out there?

Condoms are very helpful in that respect. If you don't go the condom route, then maybe you go the testing route and you both get tested before you have sex.

Of course, that route presupposes that neither one of you are currently sexually active with other partners. Do you know that about her? Have you asked? Can you trust that she's told you the truth?

Do not assume that you know the answer to that question. And know that you're taking a risk if you believe her and don't have enough experience to judge the truth of her answer.

Make a mistake on this and you may have a lifetime to remember her.

The second thing you need to think about is pregnancy. Is she on birth control? If not, are you comfortable enough to just use condoms or should you wait until she's on something?

Usually that takes time.

With birth control pills she'll need to wait until the end of her cycle and start taking them and then they aren't really effective for about a month after that. Something like an IUD needs to be inserted by the doctor, which means waiting for the appointment, and then waiting a few more days until she can have sex.

Not fun, but best to think about it now than find yourself fathering a kid with a woman you hardly know.

And, no, you are never too old to have to think about these things. I don't know where I saw it, but the 60+ age range is at the top for acquiring STDs. It's great to have fun. Just be safe about it.

WHEN TO HAVE SEX

So when should you have sex with someone you meet online?

Simple answer: Whenever you're comfortable doing so.

Now, having said that, and acknowledging that each relationship is different, in general, if you are looking for a long-term relationship, you should probably wait a few dates to have sex. Maybe even more than a few dates.

Sleep with a woman too soon and you risk flipping that switch in your brain that turns her from future mother of your children into good for a few nights. You could ruin something great if you're the type of guy to view a woman that way.

Not to mention, sex clouds your brain. When the sex is great it's easy to overlook all the ways you guys aren't compatible. All the little deal-breakers that are going to prevent this relationship from continuing already exist, but if you're in that heady glow from good sex, you'll gloss right over them.

So, as 50's housewife as it sounds, I say hold off a bit.

I would say you should wait at least three dates. In my

personal experience, that's about when men stop trying to figure out how to sleep with me and start listening to what I'm actually telling them. Up until that point they'll nod and smile about anything I say, no matter how much it contradicts what they think.

Having said that, I also don't believe in artificially stopping something that's progressing well. Don't destroy a potential relationship by setting some arbitrary limits on yourself.

Do what you're comfortable with when you're comfortable with it.

THE FIRST DATE

Here I went and talked about sex and we haven't even talked about the first date yet. I know this is a book about online dating, but that first date matters, too.

In my experience, most men default to the coffee date or drink date. It's annoying. I know some people think it's good because it lets you feel the person out without a lot of time or money committed. I get annoyed because the drink date is not really a drink date. It's a "drinks so I can see if you're worth dinner" date.

I say, be more creative. Suggest activity dates. Like a walk around a lake (in a nice public place) or bowling or pool or video games at the arcade or something that can be one or two hours but that lets you guys interact without the pressure of staring at each other trying to converse the whole time.

I'd also suggest that you pay. I know, old-school. But in my experience most men do pay. I always offer and I'm always prepared to back that offer up if needed, but I like men who pay for the first date. I think most women do.

If you're dealing with a woman who really does want

to pay, then let her pay. This is how the two scenarios work:

The check comes. You immediately or very soon after (because the place you're at will keep checking back to see if you've paid yet) reach for the check and start to pay it.

The woman should reach for her wallet and offer to pay her share.

You say, "No, I've got it."
She says, "Are you sure?"
You say, "Yes."
She says, "Thank you."
Done.

If she wants to pay, she'll say, "No, I insist" instead of "Are you sure?" If she says that, let her pay. Some women feel the need to do so. I think most appreciate if a man pays. All my friends certainly do.

I know, dating is expensive, especially if you're expected to pay. That's where creative activity dates can come in handy. You don't have to spend money to walk around a lake. And many cities have free events if it's really that hard for you.

To me paying is part of wooing a woman. I'm treated as the equal of men every day at work. When I'm dating, I want to be treated special and I want to show the man I'm with that he can do things for me, that I'm not a hundred percent independent and capable. (Although I can be.)

But that's also the type of relationship I want. Not everyone does.

So I guess you should start how you want to finish. You don't believe in doing for your woman, then don't pay. It'll certainly narrow things down quickly to just your type of woman.

CONCLUSION

That's about it. I've told you everything I can think of to help you get started. Let's see if we can't rehash it:

1. Be honest with yourself about what you want.
2. Be honest with others about what you want.
3. Be patient and persistent.
4. Be open to meeting women that aren't as attractive as you want.
5. Pick the right site or app for what you're looking for.
6. Remember people lie.
7. Align your user name/photos/profile.
8. Be yourself.
9. Avoid women who are damaged.
10. Be safe (sexually and otherwise).
11. Don't quit.

And, last, but not least, have fun with it. Good luck.

ABOUT THE AUTHOR

Cassie Leigh is a bit like that Catholic nun that used to slap your hand with a ruler when you did something wrong. Is she sweet and gentle? No. Is she effective? Yes.

She's a thirty-something woman who's been there, done that, and has a few opinions as a result. And, in her own not at all humble opinion, you'd do well to listen to her.

www.ingramcontent.com/pod-product-compliance
Lightning Source LLC
Chambersburg PA
CBHW070031040426
42333CB00040B/1532